20.00

for

ime

Edge Hill University
Learning Services

Renew Online: http://library.edgehill.ac.uk

24/7 telephone renewals: 01695 58 4333

Help line: 01695 58 4286

6 Dec '10
4 Jan '11

07 IAN 2013

Edge Hill University
W

709212

EDGE HILL UNIVERSITY	
709212	
HJ	24/04/2008
~~372.210941~~EVA	£20.00
784·624	

Credits

Author
Jean Evans

Text © Jean Evans 2005
© 2005 Scholastic Ltd

Editor
Aileen Lalor

Designed using Adobe InDesign

Assistant Editor
Kate Element

Published by Scholastic Ltd
Villiers House
Clarendon Avenue
Leamington Spa
Warwickshire
CV32 5PR

Series Designer
Anna Oliwa

Designer
Erik Ivens

www.scholastic.co.uk

Printed by Bell & Bain Ltd, Glasgow

Cover Illustration
Chris Simpson

3 4 5 6 7 8 9   7 8 9 0 1 2 3 4

Illustrations
Louise Gardner

British Library Cataloguing-in-
Publication Data
A catalogue record for this book is
available from the British Library.

Music setting
Sally Scott

All songs supplied by CYP.

ISBN 0439-96493-8
ISBN 978-0439-96493-7

The right of Jean Evans to be identified as the author of this work has been asserted by her in accordance with the Copyright, Designs and Patents Act 1988.

All rights reserved. This book is sold subject to the condition that it shall not, by way of trade or otherwise, be lent, hired out or otherwise circulated without the publisher's prior consent in any form of binding or cover other than that in which it is published and without a similar condition, including this condition, being imposed upon the subsequent purchaser.

No part of this publication or CD may be reproduced, stored in a retrieval system, or transmitted, in any form or by any means, electronic, mechanical, photocopying, recording or otherwise, without the prior permission of the publisher. This book remains copyright, although permission is granted to copy pages where indicated for classroom distribution and use only in the school which has purchased the book, or by the teacher who has purchased the book, and in accordance with the CLA licensing agreement. Photocopying permission is given only for purchasers and not for borrowers of books from any lending service.

Acknowledgement

The Qualifications and Curriculum Authority for the use of extracts from the QCA/DfEE document Curriculum Guidance for the Foundation Stage © 2000 Qualifications and Curriculum Authority.

Every effort has been made to trace copyright holders for the works reproduced in this book, and the publishers apologise for any inadvertent omissions.

Contents

Contents

Introduction

The value of circle time

Circle time should be a regular routine that all children have the opportunity to take part in. Sitting in a circle ensures that they are aware of all members of the group and can take their turn to talk and to listen. It is important to ensure that every child feels valued for their contribution, and that children respect and appreciate one another. Younger, less confident children will gain much from sharing this time with their older friends. Taking part in the experience of singing and making music together will encourage a sense of belonging and leave children with lasting memories.

How the book is organised

The CD to accompany this book features 15 lively action songs to enjoy at circle time, while the book provides a series of practical activities to support these songs. The chosen songs are a mixture of established favourites and exciting new tracks to stimulate children's interest. The book will be a valuable resource for all those working within the Foundation Stage.
The four themed chapters are:
● Nimble fingers, busy hands, featuring songs involving small finger and hand movements.
● Let's move, which extends these experiences with larger body movements.
● Sounds like fun!, introducing sound effects using percussion and everyday objects.
● Out and about, featuring songs about the outdoors.
The pages for each song include the musical score, words, suggested actions, activity ideas and a photocopiable sheet.

Using the songs to promote learning

The main activity idea for each song has been given a learning objective, consisting of a focused Stepping Stone and an overall Early Learning Goal taken from one of the six areas of learning within the Foundation Stage. All learning areas are visited and there is a good balance across them.

Stepping Stones from all of the colour bands of the Curriculum Guidance for the Foundation Stage are balanced over the whole book rather than in individual chapters, as some songs are more appropriate for younger children while others will stimulate older children. This enables practitioners to choose songs that fit comfortably into their plans for individual children.

Each activity page contains a further five activity ideas in addition to the main activity idea. An accompanying photocopiable sheet is included to support one of these activities.

Suggestions are given for the timing of the song during circle time, and for using the song to support relevant themes. Ideas for props are included where appropriate, although many of these songs require simple finger and hand movements only.

Extending opportunities

Use the songs regularly so that the children become familiar with them and can really enjoy them. It is important to maximise children's learning by encouraging them to enjoy the CD independently after the circle-time session, for example by providing a CD player that they can operate safely, a range of percussion instruments, and some puppets.

Areas of Learning

PSED Personal, social and emotional education
CLL Communication, language and literacy
MD Mathematical development
KUW Knowledge and understanding of the world
PD Physical development
CD Creative development

Nimble fingers, busy hands

We All Clap Hands Together

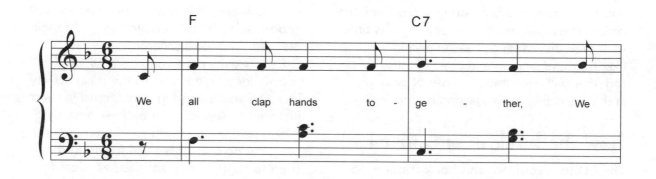

We all clap hands to - ge - ther, We

all clap hands to - ge - ther, We all clap hands to -

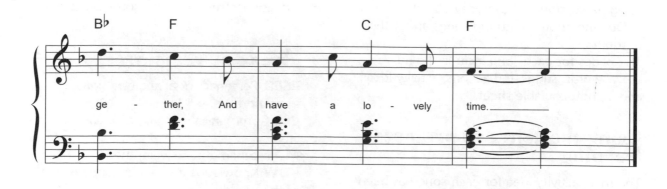

ge - ther, And have a lo - vely time.

We All Clap Hands Together

(Begin by standing in a circle facing one another.)
We all clap hands together,
We all clap hands together,
We all clap hands together,
And have a lovely time.
(Clap while singing.)

We stamp our feet together,
We stamp our feet together,
We stamp our feet together,
And have a lovely time.
(Stamp on the spot while singing.)

We jump up and down together,
We jump up and down together,
We jump up and down together,
And have a lovely time.
(Jump up and down on the spot while singing.)

We swing our arms together,
We swing our arms together,
We swing our arms together,
And have a lovely time.
(Swing both arms backwards and forwards, marching style, while singing.)

(Sing this verse more slowly)
We go to sleep together,
We go to sleep together,
We go to sleep together,
We've had a lovely time.
(Lie down, curl up and pretend to go to sleep.)

We All Clap Hands Together
How to use this song

Learning objectives

Stepping Stone
Initiate interactions with other people.

Early Learning Goal
Respond to significant experiences, showing a range of feelings when appropriate. **(PSED)**

Group size
Up to 12 children.

Sharing the song

Share this song at any time during circle time, linking with the themes of 'Healthy living' and 'All about me'.

Invite the children to hold hands and walk backwards until they form a big ring. Ask them to stand still and drop their hands against the tops of their legs. Explain that they are going to sing a song with lots of actions so they need to check that they have plenty of space. Do this by asking them to slowly stretch their arms out at their sides. If they touch another child, they are too near and need to make the circle bigger. When the children are satisfied with their personal space, invite them to sit down and listen to the song. Can they suggest suitable actions after listening to the words?

Play the track again and sing the words together, without the actions.

Stand up and practise clapping, stamping and jumping, and lying down to sleep. Talk about reasons why people clap, for example to show our support, appreciation or admiration of someone. Why would we stamp our feet?

Once the children are familiar with the words and corresponding movements, play the track a third time so that they can sing along with their actions.

Talk about how the song made them feel. Did they feel happy, excited, tired?

Finally, encourage the children to initiate interactions by working in pairs. Suggest that they stand opposite their partners and take turns to perform the actions while the other child copies.

Activity ideas

● Invite the children to pretend to be animals, composing their own verses to sing with vocal sound effects, for example, 'We squeak like mice together'. **(CLL)**
● Make copies of the photocopiable sheet and mount them on card. Cut out the pictures to form separate cards for counting and matching games. Try arranging sets of cards in the sequence they appear in the song. **(MD)**
● Make a set of action cards from the photocopiable sheet, mounting it on card and cutting out the pictures. Hold up one of the pictures, call out the action and invite the children to respond with appropriate movement. Then call out 'clap', 'jump' or 'stamp' at random, gradually increasing speed to encourage the children to enjoy more vigorous exercise. Talk about bodily changes after exercise, for example, feeling out of breath, tired and thirsty. **(PD)**

Squeak!

We All Clap Hands Together

Round and Round the Garden

Round and Round the Garden

Round and round the garden, went a teddy bear,

(Trace circles round and round the palm of a hand with the index finger of the other hand.)

One step, two step,

(Make the fingers of one hand take two steps up the other arm to the top.)

Tickle you under there.

(Move the fingers from the top of the arm to the armpit and tickle the skin. Repeat same actions as verse is repeated.)

Round and Round the Garden
How to use this song

Learning objectives

Stepping Stone
Begin to use talk instead of action to rehearse, reorder and reflect on past experience, linking significant events from own experience and from stories, paying attention to sequence and how events lead into one another.

Early Learning Goal
Use talk to organise, sequence and clarify thinking, ideas, feelings and events. **(CLL)**

Group size
Six children.

Props
The children's favourite teddy bears.

Sharing the song

Sing the song at the beginning of circle time and link to such themes as 'Bears', 'Growing', 'Feelings' and 'Babies'.

Invite the children to bring their favourite teddy for a visit and ask them to sit the teddies in the centre of the circle at circle time. Sing the song with just the finger actions as the teddies watch. Talk to the children about how the song is usually sung to babies to make them laugh.

Invite the children to sit their teddies on their knees and repeat the song, this time tracing their fingers around the palms of the teddies and then tickling them under their arms.

Suggest that the children stand up and make a large circle, each carrying their teddy bear, so that they can pretend to walk 'round and round the garden', stopping and taking two exaggerated steps forward as they sing

the words, before standing still and tickling their teddies under their arms.

Sit down again and talk about things that make the children laugh. Introduce the idea of sequence by asking what comes first, the tickle or the laugh?

Activity ideas

● Sing a selection of nursery rhymes and decide which are most suitable for babies. Prepare baby dolls for bed and sing some of the rhymes to them to help them to sleep. **(PSED)**

● Hide some teddies outdoors for the children to find. Supply directional clues such as chalk paths and arrows. Return indoors to play the board game on the photocopiable sheet. Mount the sheet onto card and invite the children to throw dice marked from 1 to 3 and move a plastic bear along the path. Every time they land on a teddy, they take a plastic bear out of a box. The aim is to collect bears and count the total at the end of the game. **(MD)**

● Make a circular obstacle course outdoors for children to negotiate with their teddies in backpacks. **(PD)**

Round and Round the Garden

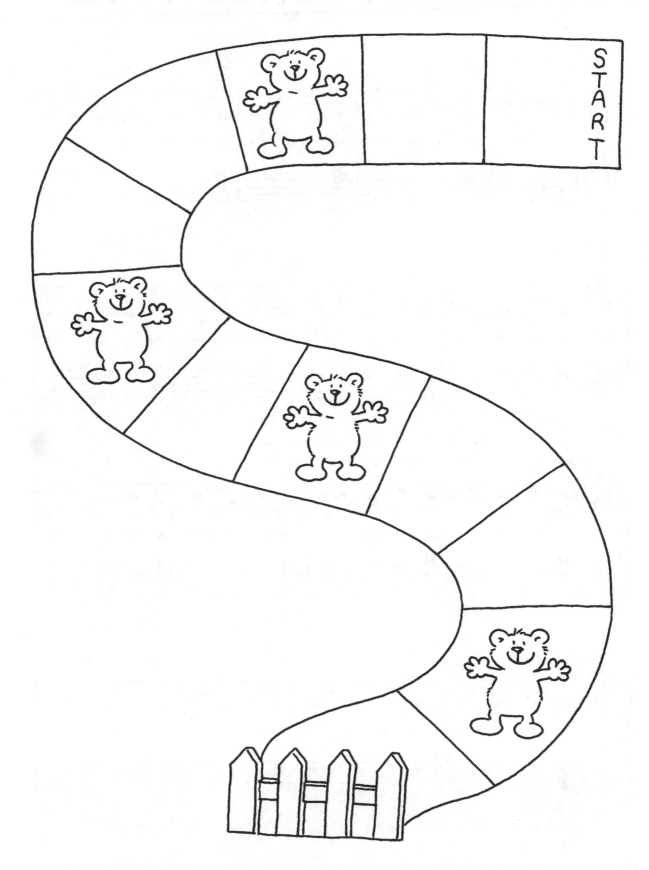

My Hands Upon my Head I Place

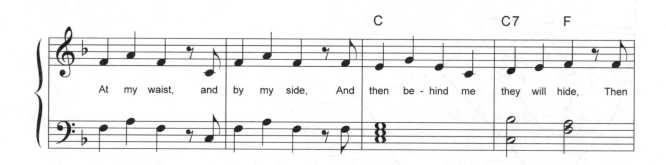

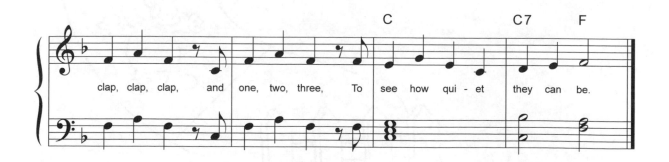

14

My Hands Upon my Head I Place

My hands upon my head I place,
(Put both hands on top of head with interlinked fingers.)

Upon my shoulders, on my face,
(Touch both shoulders, and then both cheeks.)

At my waist, and by my side,
(Put both hands on the waist at either side and then drop them down against the side of the body.)

And then behind me they will hide,
(Tuck both hands behind the back.)

Then I will raise them way up high,
(Lift both hands into the air as high as possible.)

And make my fingers fly, fly, fly,
(Move the hands from side to side above the head with the fingers wiggling.)

Then clap, clap, clap, and one, two, three,
(Clap the hands three times on the words 'clap' and then three times again while counting one, two, three.)

To see how quiet they can be.
(Hold hands together in front of the body, very still and quiet. Repeat the same actions when the verse is repeated.)

My Hands Upon my Head I Place
How to use this song

Learning objectives

Stepping Stone
Observe and use positional language.

Early Learning Goal
Use everyday words to describe position.
(MD)

Group size
Up to 12 children

Sharing the song

Link the song to themes on 'My body',
'Opposites' and 'Growing'.

Invite the children to sit in a circle and
explain that they are going to sing a song
about different parts of their bodies. Ask
them to point to their head, shoulder, face,
waist, sides, hands and fingers to make sure
that they understand the references to body
parts in the song.

Ask one of the children to touch a body
part and invite the others to copy. Move
around the circle and give each child a turn at
taking the lead with a movement for the
others to follow.

Familiarise children with the language used
in the song by explaining the word 'place' and
by introducing the positional language. Ask
them to place their hands 'upon', 'by', 'behind'
and 'high above' their heads. Show them
what is meant by 'at my side' and 'raise'. Use
a teddy bear and a box to demonstrate
'above', 'upon', 'beside' and 'inside'.

Listen to the song together and ask the
children what actions they will make. How will
they make their fingers fly? How will they
make them quiet? Suggest that they practise
their chosen actions as you say the words.
Finally, play the track, sing the words and do
the actions together.

Activity ideas

● Develop the children's concentration skills
by asking them to balance beanbags on the
body parts indicated in the song, for example,
on their face, shoulder and side. Make the
beanbags fly from side to side by holding
them up high. Extend the activity by finding
unusual places to balance the beanbag, such
as on an outstretched arm, or to hide it, such
as under a foot. **(PSED)**
● Look at the body outline on the
photocopiable sheet and help the children to
read the words and identify the parts in the
small drawings. Copy the page and mount it
on card before cutting out the drawings and
labels. Add facial features to the outline and
try putting the labels and drawings in the
right place on the body outline, giving
support to those who need it. Draw round a
child and add facial features to the outline.
Make a set of labels for the body parts
mentioned in the song. Invite the children to
put the labels in place on the outline. **(CLL)**
● Talk about how the children's hands were
'as quiet as can be' at the end of the song,
and try playing musical instruments very
loudly and then holding them still to make
them quiet. Make comparisons between loud
and quiet sounds the children have
experienced, such as balloons bursting, or
whispering. **(CD)**

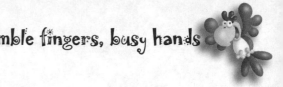

My Hands Upon my Head I Place

face		
knee		
shoulder		
foot		
hand		

Roly Poly

Roly poly, Roly poly, Roll your hands like me,

Roll them both to-ge-ther, And put them on your knee.

Ro - ly po - ly, Ro - ly Po - ly, Clap your hands like me,

Clap them both to-ge-ther, And put them on your knee.

Roly Poly

Roly poly, roly poly,
Roll your hands like me,
Roll them both together,
(Roll the hands over and over each other.)
And put them on your knee.
(Put the hands palm downwards, one on each knee.)

Roly poly, roly poly,
(Roll the hands over and over each other.)
Clap your hands like me,
Clap them both together,
(Clap the hands.)
And put them on your knee.
(Put the hands palm downwards, one on each knee.)

Roly poly, roly poly,
(Roll the hands over and over each other.)
Shake your hands like me,
Shake them both together,
(Shake both hands in front of the body.)
And put them on your knee.
(Put the hands palm downwards, one on each knee.)

Roly poly, roly poly,
(Roll the hands over and over each other.)
Wave your hands like me,
Wave them both together,
(Wave both hands above the head.)
And put them on your knee.
(Put the hands palm downwards, one on each knee.)

Roly poly, roly poly,
(Roll the hands over and over each other.)
Hide your hands like me
Hide them both together,
(Hide both hands behind the back.)
And put them on your knee.
(Bring the hands to the front of the body and put them palm downwards, one on each knee.)

Roly Poly
How to use this song

Learning objectives

Stepping Stone
Persevere in repeating some actions/attempts when developing a new skill.

Early Learning Goal
Show awareness of space, of themselves and others. **(PD)**

Group size
Up to eight children

Sharing the song

Link the song to themes on 'My body' and 'Movement'.

Invite the children to sit in a circle and explain that you are going to sing a special 'roly poly' song. Demonstrate how to roll the hands over and over each other in 'roly poly' fashion and ask the children to try, first slowly and then more quickly.

Play the song, just listening to the words. Afterwards, talk about the different movements mentioned and practise them together. Emphasise the difference between waving and shaking the hands by suggesting that the children pretend that they are waving goodbye to someone and then shaking water off their hands after washing them.

Ask the children to remain sitting to listen to the song, joining in with the words and actions when they want to. Praise their good listening skills. Play the track again so that the children can join in with increasing familiarity and enjoyment.

Once the children have mastered the skill of rolling their hands one way, suggest that they try rolling them in the opposite direction. Then challenge them to roll them backwards and forwards, starting slowly at first and then moving more quickly as their skill increases.

Activity ideas

● Make roly poly spiral snake mobiles by mounting copies of the photocopiable sheet on card and inviting the children to cut around the snake outline. Demonstrate how to create markings by drawing a zigzag line along a snake and then invite the children to make their own patterns. Provide lots of brightly coloured felt pens. Tie a length of thread to the head of each snake and hang them up to create a colourful mobile. **(CLL)**

● Put a sheet of white paper in the bottom of a shallow tray and invite the children to dip a marble into some paint and roll it across the paper by tilting the tray. Try to create 'roly poly' patterns. **(MD)**

● Help the children to create some pastry using a basic mix (you need twice as much flour as fat). Ask them to roll it into a rectangle, spread it with jam and roll it up. Cook it and allow to cool slightly before slicing. Look for the pattern on your jam roly poly as you enjoy eating it. Be aware of any food allergies and intolerances. **(KUW)**

Roly Poly

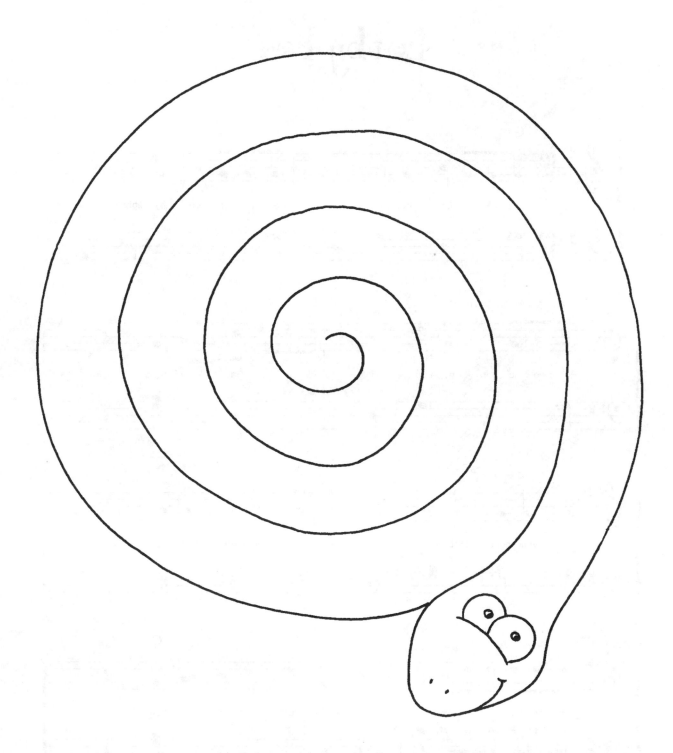

Let's move

Looby Loo

Here we go Loo - by Loo, Here we go Loo - by light,
Here we go Loo - by Loo, All on a Sa - tur - day night. You
put your right foot in, You put your right foot out,
Shake it a li - ttle a li - ttle, And turn your - self a - bout.

Looby Loo

(All stand still in the circle and clap to the beat of the introduction.)
Here we go Looby Loo,
Here we go Looby light,
Here we go Looby Loo,
(Hold hands and walk round in a circle.)
All on a Saturday night.
(Gradually come to a stop.)

You put your right foot in,
(Stand still and point right foot inside the circle.)
You put your right foot out,
(Stand still and point right foot outside the circle.)
Shake it a little a little,
(Shake right foot.)
And turn yourself about.
(Turn around once until facing inside the circle again. Join hands and repeat chorus.)

Put your left foot in,
(Stand still and point left foot inside the circle.)
Put your left foot out,
(Stand still and point left foot outside the circle.)
Shake it a little a little,
(Shake left foot.)
And turn yourself about.
(Turn around once until facing inside the circle again. Join hands and repeat chorus.)

Put your right hand in,
(Stand still and put right hand inside the circle.)
Put your right hand out,
(Stand still and put right hand behind back.)
Shake it a little a little,
(Shake right hand.)
And turn yourself about.
(Turn around until facing inside the circle again. All join hands and repeat the chorus.)

Put your left hand in,
(Stand still and put left hand inside the circle.)
And put your left hand out,
(Stand still and put left hand behind back.)
Shake it a little a little,
(Shake left hand.)
And turn yourself about.
(Turn around until facing inside the circle again. All join hands and repeat the chorus twice.)

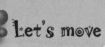
Looby Loo
How to use this song

Learning objectives

Stepping Stone
Listen to favourite nursery rhymes, stories and songs. Join in with repeated refrains, anticipating key events and important phrases.

Early Learning Goal
Listen with enjoyment, and respond to stories, songs and other music, rhymes and poems and make up their own stories, songs, rhymes and poems. **(CLL)**

Group size
At least 10 children, up to 16 maximum.

Props
Shakers.
Football rattles.
Whistles.

Sharing the song

Sing this stimulating song at the end of circle time, and use it to support work on themes such as 'Carnivals', 'Sound' and 'Opposites'. Invite the children to sit and listen to the words of the song. What or who do they think Looby Loo is? Have they ever danced at a party?

Ask the children to practise walking round in a circle together before playing the song. Play the chorus at the start of the song, and then stop the music so that the children can enjoy holding hands and walking around. Talk about left and right and ask the children to lift up their right feet. Check to make sure that all children have managed this. Play the chorus and the first verse of the song while this is fresh in their minds.

Continue playing the verses one by one, with adults evenly spread among the children.

Make sure that they are managing to distinguish left from right.

Once the children are familiar with the actions and are responding with enjoyment, sit and listen to the sound effects made with shakers, rattles and whistles. Suggest that a small group of children provide a musical accompaniment mimicking these sound effects.

Activity ideas

● Extend the children's awareness of positional language by singing 'The Hokey Cokey' with actions. **(MD)**
● Encourage the children to talk about past and present events in their lives by recalling special occasions when they have enjoyed dancing. Invite them to dress up for a special dance and play their favourite music. **(KUW)**
● Make some copies of the dancing children on the photocopiable sheet and help the children to cut them out. Invite them to draw features and clothes. Join several pairs of dancers together and then fasten them at the remaining ends to form a circle. Make them dance by moving them up and down and from side to side. **(PD)**

Looby Loo

Ring-a-ring o' Roses

Ring-a-ring o' Roses

Ring-a-ring o' roses, a pocketful of posies,
(All hold hands and dance around in a ring.)
Atishoo! Atishoo!
(Stand still, put hands in front of mouths and pretend to sneeze.)
We all fall down.
(Pretend to fall down, without holding hands.)

The cows are in the meadow,
(Get onto all fours and pretend to move like cows.)
Eating buttercups,
(All drop heads to floor, pretending to be eating buttercups.)
One, two, three!
(Sit back and clap while counting one, two, three.)
We all jump up.
(Jump up and hold hands again in a circle.)

Ring-a-ring o' Roses
How to use this song

Learning objectives

Stepping Stone
Seek out others to share experiences.

Early Learning Goal
Form good relationships with adults and peers. **(PSED)**

Group size
Up to 12 children.

Sharing the song

Sing this exciting song at the end of circle time, and use it to support work on themes such as 'Farm animals', 'Healthy Routines' and 'Shapes'.

Introduce it again during outdoor play on a soft grassy surface so that you can encourage the children to seek out others to share the experience. Suggest that older, more confident children hold the hands of those who are timid in group situations.

Stand in the middle of the grass and ask one or two children if they would like to sing the song with you again. Suggest that they go and find some friends who would like to join them in the ring. Remember to include adults as well.

Follow the given actions and then suggest making up alternative versions of the second verse, for example, with sheep on a hillside or horses in a field.

Invite the children to choose other favourite ring songs to sing such as 'The Farmer's in his Den' or 'Here We Go Round the Mulberry Bush'. Why is it easier to dance round in a circle? Try moving in the shape of a square or triangle. Move to a hard surface and draw chalk lines to define the shapes. Is it easier to dance around in a square or triangle shape now?

Activity ideas

● Make copies of the photocopiable sheet, one for each child. Ask the children to count the number of boys and girls on their sheets and then decide how many children there are altogether. Re-enact the song with the same number of small-world characters, making the girls fall down first and then counting how many girls are lying down and how many boys are standing up. Repeat with the boys falling down first. Explore different combinations of numbers to ten. **(MD)**

● Discuss the children's experiences of sneezing and emphasise good hygiene. Explain why it is important to use tissues, cover our mouths and wash our hands. Spend time practising these skills. **(PD)**

● Invite the children to follow the 'tick-tock' beat on the track with wood blocks, drums and other percussion instruments. Do the same with other songs with a regular beat, such as 'Hickory Dickory Dock'. **(CD)**

Ring-a-ring o' Roses

Everybody Shake Your Hands

FUN SONGS for the early years: Circle time

Everybody Shake Your Hands

Monday, it's Monday,
(Wave hands high in the air.)
Everybody shake your hands,
Everybody shake your hands,
(Shake both hands in front of the body with arms outstretched.)
Shake, shake, shake, shake, shake, shake, shake and shake,
(Shake both hands in time to the words.)
Everybody shake your hands,
Everybody shake your hands,
Shake, shake, shake, shake, shake, shake, shake, shake.
(As above)

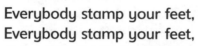

Everybody stamp your feet,
Everybody stamp your feet,
(Stamp both feet on the spot like marching soldiers.)
Stamp, stamp, stamp, stamp, stamp, stamp, stamp, stamp,
(Stamp both feet in time to the words.)
Everybody stamp your feet,
Everybody stamp your feet,
Stamp, stamp, stamp, stamp, stamp, stamp, stamp and stamp,
(As above)

Monday, it's Monday,
Monday, it's Monday,
Monday, it's Monday, woe-ooh woe.
(Wave hands in the air with arms outstretched.)

Everybody Shake Your Hands
How to use this song

Learning objectives

Stepping Stone
Manage body to create intended movements.

Early Learning Goal
Move with control and coordination. **(PD)**

Group size:
Up to 12 children.

Sharing the song

Sing this song at the start of circle time on Mondays, and use it to support work on themes such as 'Time', 'Daily routines', 'My body' and 'Opposites'.

Ask the children to name the day and explain that you would like to start the week with a happy song. Invite them to listen to the song before they practise shaking and stamping. Ask them to pretend to be mice shaking their paws gently and giants stamping with big boots. Are they aware of the contrasting movements?

Decide upon an action to associate with the word 'Monday', for example, waving their hands in the air. Ask the children to stand up to enjoy singing the song and adding the actions. Sit down again and discuss how Monday follows the weekend. Talk about how weekends are different to other days – we don't have to go to school or nursery, we might visit relatives or go out with our family. Take turns to talk about things the children and adults have enjoyed at the weekend.

Sing the song on subsequent days without using the CD, so that children can name the day and suggest a new action, for example, 'It's Tuesday, everybody wiggle your hips', or 'It's Wednesday, everybody nod your head'.

Activity ideas

● Copy the photocopiable sheet, mount the pictures on card and cut them out. Hold up the cards at random, shouting 'stamp' or whispering 'scamper'. Invite the children to stamp around heavily when they see the giant, and scamper along lightly when they see the mouse. Beat a drum loudly and tap a triangle softly to create contrasting sounds. Which sound would the giant make? Ask the children to think of times when they have been angry and times when they are very happy. Suggest that they make up dances for these contrasting feelings as they hear the instruments. **(PSED)**
● Share with the children books about opposites, for example, *Shark Goes Zoom!* from the *Bang on the Door* series (Oxford University Press). **(CLL)**
● Develop children's awareness of the passing of time by creating a 'Days of the week' chart for them to fill in, with drawings and captions about their chosen action for the song on each day. **(KUW)**
● Transfer the shaking and stamping actions into creative work by showing the children how to shake a paintbrush to make splatter paintings, and how to dip the sole of a shoe into paint and stamp it onto a length of paper to make exciting prints. **(CD)**

Everybody Shake Your Hands

Hands on Hips

Hands on hips, ___ Hands on knees, ___

Hands be - hind you, If you please. ___

Touch your shoul - ders, Touch your toes, ___

Touch your knees, ___ And then touch your nose. ___

Raise your hands, ___ way up high, ___ Let your fin - gers, swift - ly fly. ___

Hold them out, ___ in front of you, ___ While you clap them, one and two. ___

Hands on Hips

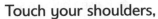

Hands on hips,
(Place one hand on each hip.)
Hands on knees,
(Place one hand on each knee.)
Hands behind you,
(Put both hands behind backs.)
If you please.
(Move one outstretched finger backwards and forwards, pointing to the others in the group.)

Touch your shoulders,
(Place one hand on each shoulder.)
Touch your toes,
(Bend down and touch toes.)
Touch your knees,
(Place one hand on each knee.)
And then touch your nose.
(Touch the nose with index finger.)

Raise your hands, way up high,
(Lift hands up straight above head.)
Let your fingers swiftly fly.
(Move the hands from side to side while wiggling the fingers.)
Hold them out in front of you,
(Hold the hands out in front of the body, wiggling the fingers.)
While you clap them, one and two.
(Clap the hands twice in time to the words. Repeat twice from beginning of song, getting gradually faster.)

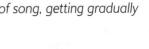

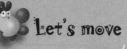
Hands on Hips
How to use this song

Learning objectives

Stepping Stone
Describe simple features of objects and events.

Early Learning Goal
Find out about, and identify, some features of living things, objects and events they observe. **(KUW)**

Group size
Up to 12 children.

Sharing the song

This action song is an ideal way to start or end a circle time session and can be used to support work on themes such as 'My body', 'Living things' and 'Opposites'.

Ask the children to stand in a circle facing one another and invite them to point to their hips, knees, shoulders, toes and nose to ensure that they are all aware of the different body parts mentioned in the song. Give support to those who need it. Explain the meaning of the word 'swift' and discuss how the children might make their fingers 'swiftly fly'. Suggest they practise making their fingers fly high and low, in front of and behind their bodies.

Play the song and model the actions to support the children as they join in. Recall the different parts of their bodies that the children have used in the song. Invite them to think of living things they are familiar with. Consider the features of these creatures. Does a monkey have a nose? Does a cat have knees and shoulders? Does a fish have toes and fingers?

Talk about features that the children do not have, such as fins, a trunk, or wings, and invite them to imagine what it would be like to swim with fins, use a trunk to pick things up, or fly with wings. Suggest that they find a space and pretend to be fish, elephants or birds.

Activity ideas

● Encourage the children to listen and to respond to instructions by playing 'Simon says'. **(PSED)**
● Raise children's awareness of the importance of exercise by suggesting that they take part in a sports day. Invite them to dress appropriately in shorts and T-shirts and organise fun activities, such as hopping and jumping around obstacles. Stress the importance of warming up and cooling down before and after vigorous exercise. **(PD)**
● Ask the children to recall how they made their fingers fly by flapping them and then follow the instructions on the photocopiable sheet to create bird finger puppets from scrap materials. Sing the rhyme 'Two little Dicky Birds' and make the puppets fly. **(CD)**

Hands on Hips

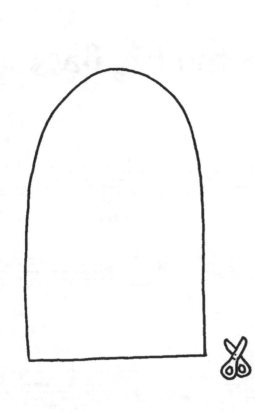

What you need

- Brightly coloured felt
- Scissors
- Blunt needle with large eye
- Strong thread
- PVA glue
- Glue spreaders
- Fabric scraps
- Buttons, sequins or small plastic eyes

What you do

- Make two copies of the template for each child and cut around the thick black lines.
- Invite children to choose the colour of felt they would like to use. Pin two of the templates to each child's chosen felt and cut around them. Place the two pieces together.
- Demonstrate to more able children how to sew around the edge of the felt using a simple running stitch. Leave the straight edge at the bottom of the puppet open. Invite less able children to put a thin layer of glue around the edge of the felt, again leaving the straight edge open, and show them how to press the two edges together to form the puppet. Allow the glue to dry.
- Create a beak from a triangle of yellow fabric and glue on plastic eyes, sequins or buttons.
- Encourage the children to personalise their puppets by adding small scraps of fabric or wool of their choice.

Sounds like fun!

Oh, We Can Play on the Big Bass Drum

O - h, we can play on the big bass drum, And

this is the way we do it, Boom, boom, boom on the

big bass drum. And that's the way we do it.

Oh, We Can Play on the Big Bass Drum

Oh, we can play on the big bass drum,
And this is the way we do it,
Boom, boom, boom on the big bass
drum.
And that's the way we do it.
*(Pretend to play a big bass drum, holding the drum
up in the air with one hand and beating it sideways
with the other.)*

Oh, we can play on the silver flute,
And this is the way we do it,
Toot, toot, toot on the silver flute,
And that's the way we do it.
*(Pretend to play a flute, holding it sideways near
the mouth and moving the fingers up and down to
play the notes.)*

Oh, we can play on the triangle,
And this is the way we do it,
Ting, ting, ting on the triangle,
And that's the way we do it.
*(Pretend to play a triangle, holding it with one
hand and beating it with the other.)*

*(Pretend to play any of the above instruments
while the music plays between these verses.)*

Oh, we can play on the instruments,
And this is way we do it,
Play, play, play on the instruments,
And that's the way we do it.
(Pretend to play one of the above instruments.)

Oh, We Can Play on the Big Bass Drum
How to use this song

Learning objectives

Stepping Stone
Explore the different sounds of instruments.

Early Learning Goal
Recognise and explore how sounds can be changed, sing simple songs from memory, recognise repeated sounds and sound patterns and match movements to music. **(CD)**

Group size
Up to 12 children.

Props
A picture of someone marching with a bass drum.
A flute, or a picture of one, and a plastic bottle.
Four large drums and four beaters.
Four cardboard tubes.
Foil.
Four triangles and four beaters.

Sharing the song

Enjoy this exciting song towards the end of circle time, and use it to support work on themes such as 'Sound', 'Carnivals' and 'Festivals'.

Listen to the song together before discussing the instruments mentioned. Look at a picture of a big bass drum and talk about how the drummer in a marching band has straps to hold the drum in place and a large beater to create a booming sound.

Ask the children to march in a circle pretending to play big bass drums. Show them a flute, or a picture of one. Play a note if possible, and explain how pressing the keys on the flute creates different notes. Demonstrate blowing across the top of a bottle filled with water, and change the volume of water to change the note. Ask the children to play imaginary flutes, singing 'toot, toot, toot' as they do so.

Pass around a triangle, hit it and discuss the sound it makes. Invite the children to beat imaginary triangles, singing 'ting, ting, ting' as they do so.

Play the song, marching around in a circle, singing the words and following the suggested actions. Share out the drums, triangles and beaters, and flutes created from cardboard tubes covered in foil. March around with the instruments while singing the song, making comparisons between the different sounds made.

Activity ideas

● Create an instrument matching game with eight copies of the photocopiable sheet. Mount the copies on card. Keep four to form activity boards and cut the rest into picture cards. Give four children a board each and hold up cards at random for them to match to a picture on their board. Extend the activity by listening to or looking at real instruments instead of using picture cards. **(PSED)**
● Invite the children to make up their own verses to the song, choosing from a wider range of instruments. **(CLL)**
● Raise the children's community awareness by inviting local musicians to come in and play different instruments to them, ideally from a range of cultures. **(KUW)**
● Take a selection of instruments outside along with a battery-operated CD player and some recordings of military band music. Encourage the children to march to the music, playing their chosen instruments. **(PD)**

Oh, We Can Play on the Big Bass Drum

I Hear Thunder

I hear thun - der, I hear thun - der, Hark! don't you?

Hark! don't you? Pi - tter, pa - tter rain - drops, Pi - tter, pa - tter rain - drops,

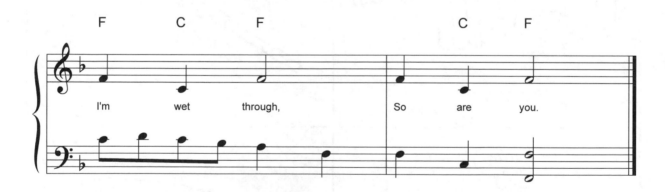

I'm wet through, So are you.

I Hear Thunder

I hear thunder,
I hear thunder,
(Cup a hand behind the ear and look upwards, pretending to listen.)
Hark! don't you?
Hark! don't you?
(Do the same, but using the other hand.)
Pitter, patter raindrops,
Pitter, patter raindrops.
(Wiggle the fingers while moving the hands up and down in front of the body.)
I'm wet through,
(Wrap arms around the body and pretend to shiver.)
So are you.
(Point to another child. Repeat the actions as the verse is repeated.)

I Hear Thunder
How to use this song

Learning objectives

Stepping Stone
Show an awareness of change.

Early Learning Goal
Look closely at similarities, differences, patterns and change. **(KUW)**

Group size
6 children.

Props
Drums.
Cymbals.
Rainmakers.
Triangles.
Homemade shakers.
Wood blocks.

Sharing the song

This popular song can be sung when discussing the weather at the start of circle time on a wet or stormy day. It can also be used to support work on themes such as 'Weather', 'Changes', 'Clothes' and 'Seasons'.

Follow your usual routine of filling in a weather chart or discussing weather conditions. Tell the children that you have a special weather song and listen to it together.

Talk about how we use our ears to listen, and explain that some people cup a hand behind an ear to help them to hear better. Suggest that they try doing this while you walk around and whisper something to each child. Could they hear your whispers? Explain that 'hark' means the same as 'listen'.

Discuss the sound that raindrops make. If possible, go outside and stand under umbrellas to listen to the 'pitter patter' sound as the rain hits the surface.

Invite the children to recall times when

they have been wet through. How did they feel? Were they cold and uncomfortable? How did they warm up?

Practise the suggested actions and then play the song and join in with the words and actions. Show the children the selection of instruments and play each one while they listen. Which instrument would be most suitable for the sound of thunder? What can the children use to create raindrop sounds? Choose two children to create the sound of thunder and rain on their chosen instruments while the rest of the children sing and do the actions.

Activity ideas

● Use instruments to create the sound of loud thunder to stimulate discussion about children's experiences of storms. How did they feel when they heard thunder rumbling and saw flashes of lightning? Dispel fears by explaining the cause of thunder and lightning **(PSED)**
● Provide a range of rainwear and waterproof materials such as umbrellas and wellies for them to explore. Talk about when they need to wear them and why. Show children a range of different materials, such as denim, cotton, plastic and rubber and ask which they think might make the best rainhat. Provide some waterproof material and invite them to try to make a rainhat for a doll. Test by pouring water from a watering can over the doll's head to see if her hair stays dry.**(CLL)**
● Invite the children to put on appropriate clothes for wet weather from a selection of different garments. Extend this activity by making copies of the photocopiable sheet, mounting them on card and cutting out the small pictures to create individual cards. Sort the cards into two piles of clothes, suitable for hot, dry weather and cold, wet weather. **(PD)**
● Have fun jumping in puddles wearing wellies, coats and rainhats in outdoor play. **(CD)**

I Hear Thunder

Peter Hammers with One Hammer

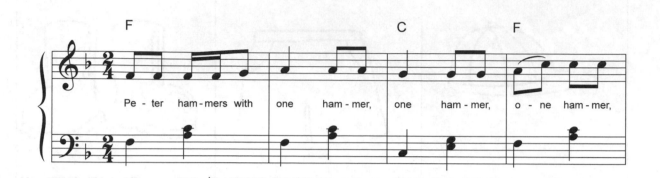

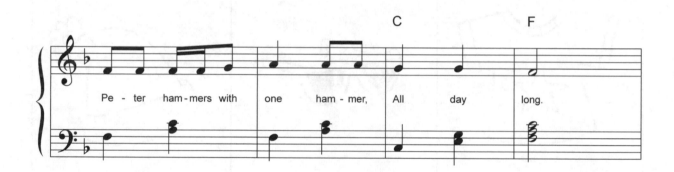

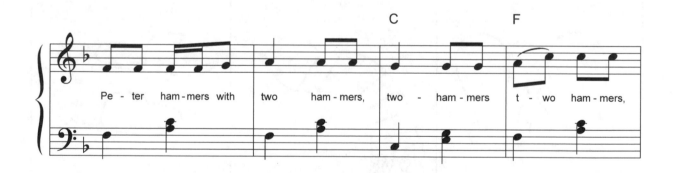

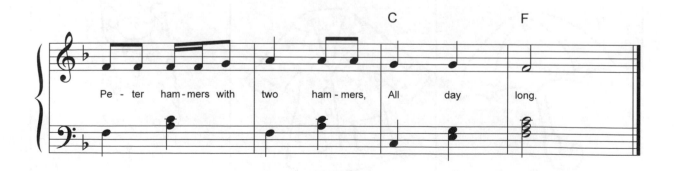

Peter Hammers with One Hammer

(Sit in a circle with the legs stretched out in front of the body.)
Peter hammers with one hammer, one hammer, one hammer,
Peter hammers with one hammer,
All day long.
(Tap on one leg with one fist in time to the beat.)

Peter hammers with two hammers, two hammers, two hammers,
Peter hammers with two hammers,
All day long.
(Tap on both legs with both fists in time to the beat.)

Peter hammers with three hammers, three hammers, three hammers,
Peter hammers with three hammers,
All day long.
(Tap on both legs with both fists, and lift one leg up and down against the floor, in time to the beat.)

Peter hammers with four hammers, four hammers, four hammers,
Peter hammers with four hammers,
All day long.
(Tap on both legs with both fists, and lift both legs up and down against the floor, in time to the beat.)

Peter hammers with five hammers, five hammers, five hammers,
Peter hammers with five hammers,
All day long.
(Tap on both legs with both fists, lift both legs up and down against the floor and nod the head in time to the beat.)

Peter's very tired now, tired now, tired now,
Peter's very tired now
All day long.
(Stretch both arms into the air, yawn and curl up, pretending to sleep.)

Peter's wide awake now, awake now, awake now,
Peter's wide awake now
All day long.
(Jump up quickly to a standing position.)

Peter Hammers with One Hammer

How to use this song

Learning objectives

Stepping Stone
Count up to three or four objects by saying one number name for each item.

Early Learning Goal
Count reliably up to 10 everyday objects. **(MD)**

Group size
Up to 10 children.

Sharing the song

This counting song can be sung at any time during circle time and can be used to support themes such as 'Counting rhymes', 'Occupations', 'Daily routines' and 'How things work'.

Ask the children to sit with their legs stretched in front of them as they listen to the song. What do they think Peter is doing? Is he mending or making something?

Suggest that the children make a fist to represent a hammer and practise hammering on one leg. Can they make two hammers? Demonstrate how to hammer with two fists while lifting one leg up and down for three hammers, and then both legs for four hammers. Finally, nod the head to make the fifth hammer. Count loudly and distinctly as you practise the actions to familiarise the children with the sequence.

Discuss how Peter would feel after a hard day's work and pretend to curl up and go to sleep. Talk about how the children feel after a sleep. Do they jump out of bed feeling wide awake, like Peter does?

Play the song, sing the words and introduce the suggested actions. Once the children are familiar with the song, pause the CD after each verse to count the hammers.

Activity ideas

● Raise the children's awareness of the codes for safe behaviour by introducing them to simple rules for handling hammers and nails. Demonstrate how you can hammer nails into a piece of wood and then wind string around the nails to form different patterns. **(PSED)**
● Increase the children's vocabulary using the photocopiable sheet. Make copies of the whole page and invite the children to try to name the tools before cutting around their thick outlines and gluing them to the matching silhouettes in Peter's box. Handle some real tools safely and try to name them and match them to the tools in Peter's box. **(CLL)**
● Provide the children with a wide range of twigs, small branches, logs and scrap pieces of wood to explore and invite them to make models with them. **(KUW)**

Peter Hammers with One Hammer

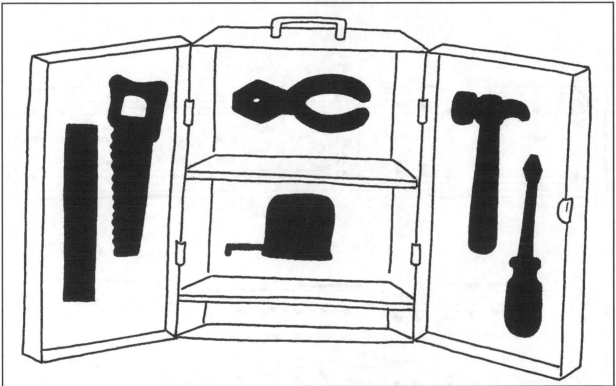

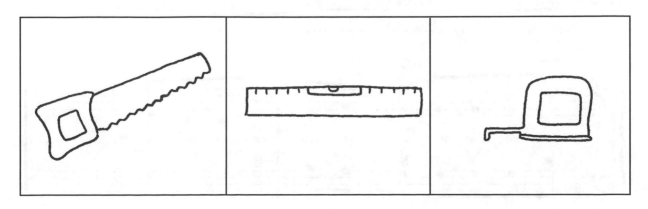

Out and about

Dingle Dangle Scarecrow

When all the co-ws were slee-ping, And the

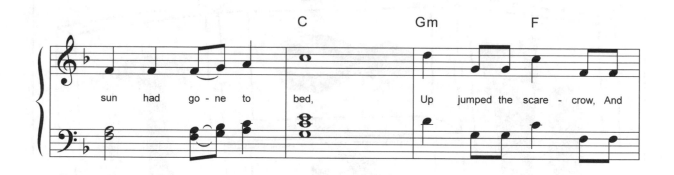

sun had go-ne to bed, Up jumped the scare-crow, And

this is what he said, I'm a din-gle dan-gle scare-crow, With a fli-ppy flo-ppy hat, I can

shake my hands like this, I can shake my feet like that.

Dingle Dangle Scarecrow

(Sit down and make the sound of crows cawing during the introductory music.)

When all the cows were sleeping,
(Curl up on the floor pretending to be cows sleeping.)
And the sun had gone to bed,
(Tilt head upwards to look for the sun.)
Up jumped the scarecrow,
And this is what he said,
(Jump up and wave arms in the air.)
I'm a dingle dangle scarecrow,
With a flippy floppy hat,
(Nod head from side to side with hands on hips.)
I can shake my hands like this,
(Shake hands in front of the body.)
I can shake my feet like that.
(Shake one foot at a time, out to the side of the body.)

When all the hens were roosting,
(Squat on the floor pretending to be hens roosting on a perch.)
And the moon behind a cloud,
(Tilt head upwards to look for the moon.)
Up jumped the scarecrow,
(Jump up and wave arms in the air.)
And shouted very loud,
I'm a dingle dangle scarecrow,
With a flippy floppy hat,
(Nod head from side to side with hands on hips, shouting the words of the song loudly.)
I can shake my hands like this,
(Shake hands in front of the body.)
I can shake my feet like that.
(Shake one foot at a time, out to the side of the body.)

(Make the sound of crows cawing during the music at the end of the song.)

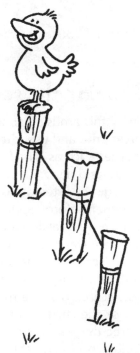

Dingle Dangle Scarecrow
How to use this song

Learning objectives

Stepping Stone
Develop a repertoire of actions by putting a sequence of movements together.

Early Learning Goal
Use their imagination in music and dance. **(CD)**

Group size
Up to 12 children.

Props
Pictures of scarecrows.

Sharing the song

Enjoy this amusing song towards the end of circle time and use it to support work on themes such as 'The farm', 'Country life' and 'Night and day'.

Begin by listening to the words of the song together before looking at the scarecrow pictures and talking about them. Have the children ever seen a scarecrow? Does the word 'scarecrow' help them to understand its purpose? Is it possible to tell from the pictures how scarecrows are made?

Ask the children to consider how the scarecrow might move. Explain that 'dingle dangle' probably refers to the way the scarecrow hangs from a frame and blows in the wind. Talk about how the scarecrow has a 'flippy, floppy' hat. Invite the children to try out 'shaky', 'dangly' and 'floppy' movements before playing the song again so that they can introduce their chosen movements.

Discuss the other characters in the song, the cows and hens, and create actions for them. Refer to the suggested actions if necessary.

Once the children are familiar with the words and actions, ask for volunteers to be the scarecrow, hens and cows and repeat the song.

Activity ideas

● Transform the home area into a farmhouse and stand a large model scarecrow outside. Create the scarecrow from old clothes stuffed with straw. Make the head by covering a balloon with pasted paper strips, allowing it to dry and then painting it. Stick on fabric features and add straw hair and a hat. Tie the scarecrow body over a T-shaped wooden frame and push the head onto the top. Stand the whole thing in a bucket of sand. Hang crow mobiles made from black card above the area. **(CLL)**
● Create scarecrow masks by making copies of the photocopiable sheet and mounting them on card. Invite the children to paint them, cut them out and add collage materials such as straw hair and whiskers, or button eyes. **(KUW)**
● Use recycled plastic containers and various grains to create shakers to accompany the song. **(PD)**

Dingle Dangle Scarecrow

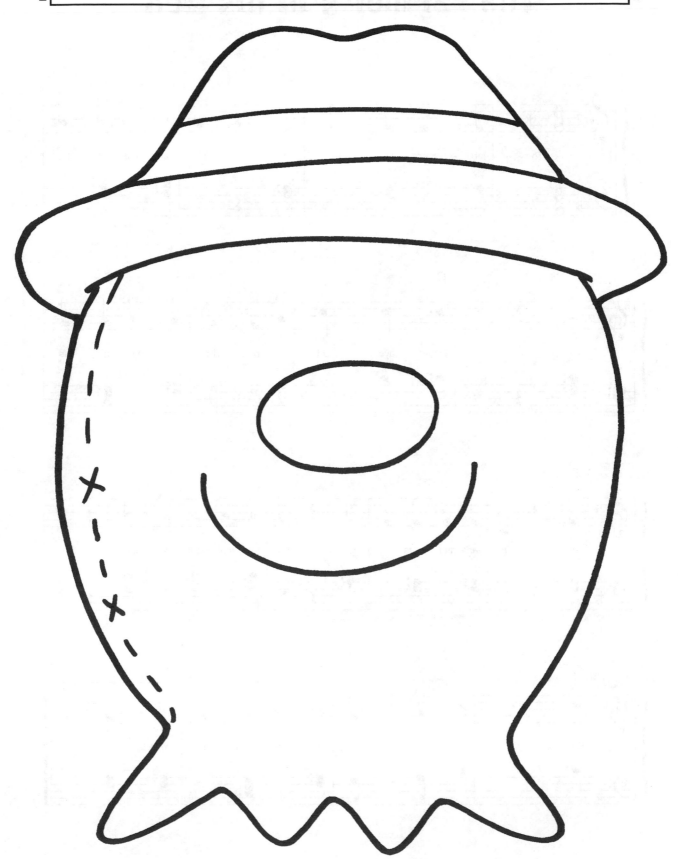

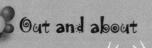

The Farmer's in his Den

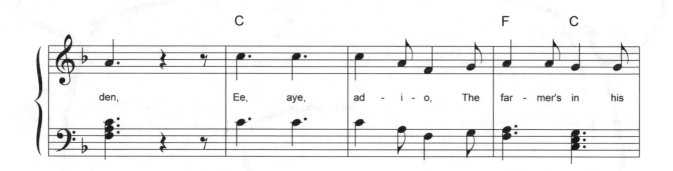

The far-mer's in his den, The far-mer's in his
den, Ee, aye, ad-i-o, The far-mer's in his

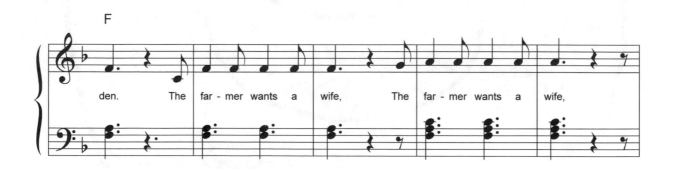

den. The far-mer wants a wife, The far-mer wants a wife,

Ee, aye, ad-i-o, The far-mer wants a wife.____

The Farmer's in his Den

(Hold hands in a ring and put in the centre appropriate hats for all of the characters, except the dog. Choose a child to be the farmer to go into the ring and put on the farmer's hat.)

The farmer's in his den,
The farmer's in his den,
Ee, aye, adio,
The farmer's in his den.

(Dance around the farmer, holding hands.)

The farmer wants a wife,
The farmer wants a wife,
Ee, aye, adio,
The farmer wants a wife.

(The children dance around during the verse. At the end, the farmer chooses a wife by pointing. The wife goes into the centre of the ring, puts on an appropriate hat, holds the farmer's hand and dances around.)

The wife wants a child,
The wife wants a child,
Ee, aye, adio,
The wife wants a child.

(The children dance around during the verse. At the end, the wife chooses a 'child' by pointing. The 'child' goes into the centre of the ring, puts on an appropriate hat, holds the other characters' hands and dances around.)

The child wants a nurse,
The child wants a nurse,
Ee, aye, adio,
The child wants a nurse.

(The children dance around during the verse. At the end, the 'child' chooses a nurse by pointing. The nurse goes into the centre of the ring, puts on an appropriate hat, holds the other characters' hands and dances around.)

The nurse wants a dog,
The nurse wants a dog,
Ee, aye, adio,
The nurse wants a dog.

(The children dance around during the verse and at the end the nurse chooses a dog by pointing. The dog goes into the centre of the ring, holds the other characters' hands and dances around.)

The dog wants a bone,
The dog wants a bone,
Ee, aye, adio,
The dog wants a bone.

(The children dance around during the verse. At the end, the dog chooses a bone by pointing. The bone goes into the centre of the ring.)

We all pat the bone,
We all pat the bone,
Ee, aye, adio,
The dog wants a bone.

(All the characters walk around the bone, patting it very gently. The last verse is repeated.)

The Farmer's in his Den
How to use this song

Learning objectives

Stepping Stone
Remember and talk about significant things that have happened to them.

Early Learning Goal
Find out about past and present events in their own lives, and those of their families and other people they know. **(KUW)**

Group size
12 children.

Props
Suitable hats for a farmer, farmer's wife, child and nurse.

Sharing the song

Enjoy this song as a ring game at the end of circle time, and use it to support work on themes such as 'The farm', 'My family' and 'All about me'.

Listen to the song together before talking about the farmer's family. How many children does the farmer have? Are there any pets in the song? Explain that the nurse is there to look after the child, not because he/she is ill. Make clear the role of a children's nurse by discussing the children's experiences of carers such as childminders.

Make comparisons with the children's families. Do they have any brothers or sisters? Are any of them only children? Introduce different family groups, such as single parent families and families with stepchildren. Be sensitive to individual circumstances.

Talk about important family events, such as weddings and the births of younger siblings. Introduce family celebrations related to cultures and beliefs. Sensitively discuss the

loss of close relatives if this arises.

Introduce the hats and ask the children to guess which characters will wear them. Sing the song as a ring game following the suggested actions. If any of the children dislike the idea of being patted, substitute the word 'clap' for 'pat' if they are chosen to be the bone at the end of the song.

Activity ideas

● Invite the children to paint or draw pictures of their families and talk about the different family members depicted. Create a display about 'Our families', using photographs and the children's pictures with appropriate captions. Once again, be sensitive to circumstances. **(PSED)**
● Make a copy of the photocopiable sheet, mount it on card and cut out the pictures of the characters from the song. Invite the children to colour the cards. Develop their awareness of sequence by asking them to arrange the cards in order as they listen to the song. **(MD)**
● Transform your home area into the farmer's house by including clothes and props for the different characters in the song. **(CD)**

The Farmer's in his Den

See-saw Margery Daw

See-saw Margery Daw

(Sit on the floor with a partner with feet touching and join hands. Rock backwards and forwards in time to the introductory music.)

See-saw, Margery Daw,
Johnny shall have a new master,
He shall have but a penny a day,
Because he can't go any faster.

(Continue to rock in pairs while singing the song.)

(Continue the actions as the verse is repeated twice.)

See-saw Margery Daw
How to use this song

Learning objectives

Stepping Stone
Show awareness of rhyme and alliteration.

Early Learning Goal
Link sounds to letters, naming and sounding the letters of the alphabet. **(CLL)**

Group size
Six children.

Props
See-saw or rocking boat.

Sharing the song

Enjoy this relaxing song at any time during circle time, and use it to support work on themes such as 'Friends', 'Toys', 'How things work' and 'Opposites'.

Show the children the see-saw or rocking boat and let them take turns to come and ride on it. Can they explain how they made it move up and down? Talk about the children's experiences of see-saws or rocking boats.

Explain that you have a song about playing on a see-saw, and suggest that the children pretend to be on see-saws with their friends as they sing it. Invite them to choose a partner to sit beside while they listen to the song and show them how to sit opposite one another with their feet touching. Allow time for the children to practise holding hands with their partners and rocking backwards and forwards together, pretending to be on a see-saw, before they try singing the song as well.

Ask the children to listen for the names of the two children riding the see-saw in the song, Margery Daw and Johnny. Try substituting the names of the children as each

pair takes a turn to do the actions while the others watch, one pair for each of the three verses.

Raise awareness of initial letter sounds by asking the children to say the first letter sound in their names. Can they say what sounds Margery and Johnny begin with?

Encourage the children to be aware of rhyme and alliteration by emphasising the rhyming words, 'saw' and 'Daw', 'master' and 'faster', while they are rocking. Explain the word 'rhyme' and try to find other rhyming words in favourite nursery rhymes.

Activity ideas

● Extend opportunities for the children to work together by singing 'Row, row, row your boat' with similar actions. **(PSED)**
● Encourage children to investigate balance by using a rocker scale or bucket balance as a see-saw for small toys. **(MD)**
● Develop design and technology skills by asking the children to make see-saws for small world characters using recycled scrap materials. **(KUW)**
● Give children copies of the photocopiable sheet and invite them to cut out the pictures. Can they find the rhyming pairs? Suggest that they play a game of 'Snap'.**(PD)**

See-saw Margery Daw

Here's the Church, Here is the Steeple

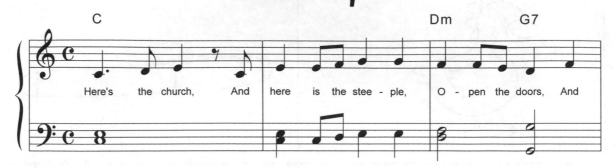

Here's the Church, Here is the Steeple

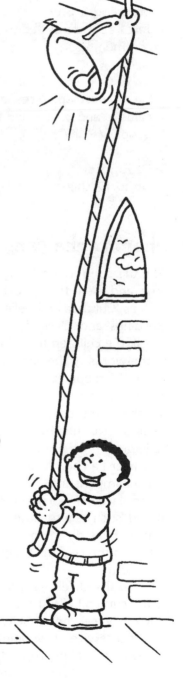

(Stand in a circle pretending to pull big ropes to the sound of the church bells during the song introduction.)

Here's the church,
(Stand still and hold both arms up high above the head.)

And here is the steeple,
(Remain standing still with both arms held high above the head, and press both hands together, palms facing, to form a pointed steeple.)

Open the doors,
(Open both arms wide as if opening doors.)

And here are the people,
(Point to the rest of the children around the circle.)

Here is the parson,
Going upstairs,
(Pretend to climb upstairs on the spot, moving arms to indicate holding banisters.)

And here he is,
Saying his prayers.
(Kneel down and put both hands together as if in prayer.)

(Repeat the actions as the verse is repeated twice.)

Here he is, here he is,
Here he is, saying his prayers,
Here he is, saying his prayers,
Saying his prayers.
(Stay on knees with both hands together.)

Here's the Church, Here is the Steeple
How to use this song

Learning objectives

Stepping Stone
Talk freely about their home and community.

Early Learning Goal
Have a developing respect for their own cultures and beliefs and those of other people. **(PSED)**

Group size
Up to 12 children.

Sharing the song

Sing this song as a calming welcome to circle time, and use it to support work on themes such as 'Cultures and beliefs', 'Out and about', 'Buildings' and 'Occupations'.

Ask the children to sit in a circle and listen to the words of the song. Explain the words 'parson', 'steeple' and 'prayers' and discuss the children's own experiences of places of worship in the community. Do any of them go to a local church? Can they describe the building and when they attend? Have they ever heard a church choir or a loud organ? Make comparisons between churches and other places of worship the children might attend, such as a mosque, synagogue or temple. How do the building shapes vary? What do the children's experiences have in common?

Draw the children's attention to the sound of the church bells at the start of the song. Have they ever heard bells chiming, perhaps before a service or wedding? Explain how bell-ringers pull big ropes to make the bells in the tall church tower chime, and talk about how complicated the routines are.

Sing the song together and follow the suggested actions.

Activity ideas

● Visit a local place of worship and obtain permission for the children to enjoy sensory exploration by looking at patterns in stained glass; gently touching carvings, fabrics and stonework; listening for bells chiming, an organ playing or a choir singing; describing the different smells such as flowers and polish. Talk about the experience on return. **(CLL)**

● Develop small finger skills by building a church with a steeple and seats from recycled materials. Introduce small world people to represent the parson, choir and congregation. **(PD)**

● Create some large stained glass windows from coloured tissue paper or cellophane glued to black paper outlines. Make smaller frames using rectangles of card. Cut out the centre of the rectangle to leave a surrounding frame. Invite the children to glue tissue paper or coloured cellophane to the back. Fasten the large and small frames to a window to let the light shine through. **(CD)**